MW00940327

The Biblical Foundations of Instrumental Music in Worship

Four Pillars

Brian L. Hedrick

Outskirts Press, Inc.
Denver, Colorado

To Mellonee
my partner in ministry and life

More Praise for

THE BIBLICAL FOUNDATIONS OF INSTRUMENTAL MUSIC IN WORSHIP: FOUR PILLARS:

Brian Hedrick has combined and distilled a great deal of vital material. This book is a must read (and often, at that) for everyone involved in instrumental ministry – player and director alike. The biblical and theological information clearly explains the foundation for what God has called us to do. We see in the histories that God has ordained and sustained instrumental music in His church – as it will be with Him in Heaven!

Jeff Cranfill, Minister of Instrumental Music
First Baptist Church, Atlanta, Georgia

Brian Hedrick is to be commended for his comprehensive and accurate justification for the use of instrumental music in contemporary worship. This scholarly work is of great benefit to church instrumentalists, their directors and church musicians everywhere!

John Gage, Minister of Instrumental Music
Valley Baptist Church, Bakersfield, California

Instrumental Music in the church has provided a unique vitality in worship for centuries. Brian

Hedrick has done a masterful job of illuminating the history and the biblical basis for instrumental music in worship. He has also offered wonderful insights that will challenge instrumentalists to use their talents more completely for the glory of God. This book is a "must read" for anyone involved in the use of instrumental music in worship.

Camp Kirkland
Church music arranger and orchestrator
Nashville, Tennesse

In this writing, Dr. Hedrick has brought a very concise, interesting, and positive historical and theological overview on the use of instruments in worship of God. It should give great encouragement to all those who are involved in this important ministry in today's church.

Dr. A. Joseph King
Retired Professor of Church Music
Southwestern Baptist Theological Seminary

As important as music is in the context of evangelical worship services today, every minister of music and church musician would do well to read this book. Through his "Four Pillars," Brian Hedrick has given us an approachable and biblical basis for better understanding the place of instrumental music in worship.

Dr. Michael D. Sharp, Professor of Worship Studies
New Orleans Baptist Theological Seminary

Contents

Acknowledgement

The subject matter of this book was originally a major part of my doctoral thesis at the Robert E. Webber Institute for Worship Studies. This work likely would not have been accomplished, nor would I have been enrolled at the Institute for Worship Studies, if it were not for the recommendation and encouragement of Dr. A. Joseph King. Not only was Dr. King a tremendous influence on my formation while I was at Southwestern Baptist Theological Seminary in the early 80s, but after twenty years of ministry, when I asked his advice on possible doctoral programs, he suggested I consider the program at I.W.S. I am also indebted to him, and the four other biblical and musical scholars who have encouraged me in this project: my supervisor, Dr. Andrew Hill (Wheaton College), Dr. Douglas Smith (Southern Baptist Theological Seminary), Dr. Allen Lott (Southwestern Baptist Theological Seminary), and Dr. William Lane Craig, noted apologist and a member of Johnson Ferry Baptist Church, where I serve as Minister of Instrumental Music.

Of course, I am extremely grateful for the support and participation of the members of the

Metro Instrumental Directors Conference, who were the original recipients of this material. We all are part of a unique Christian fraternity, and I hope the devotional series has encouraged and inspired each of you, as you serve the Lord in the ministry of instrumental music.

Finally, I would like to thank my wife, Mellonee, my family, and the elders, staff, and congregation of Johnson Ferry Baptist Church for allowing me to pursue my Doctorate in Worship Studies. I am especially grateful to my pastor, Bryant Wright, and my boss, Mark Cottingham, for encouraging me to seek my doctorate, and consequently, giving me the opportunity to write on something that is truly a passion in my life.

Soli Deo Gloria!
Brian L. Hedrick
November 2008

Foreword

Church instrumentalists who read this book should have no real surprises. We who have spent much of our lives performing in church rarely feel a need to justify our efforts. What Brian Hedrick has given us, in a scholarly, yet very interesting form, is a history of instruments used in worship that extends well into the Old Testament.

Dr. Hedrick's book is constructed on four "pillars," two from the Old Testament, with King David playing the prominent role, and two from the New. We instrumentalists claim plenty of Old Testament credibility for our work, but alas, the New Testament is much more limited, and there are those who are inclined to forbid elements merely because they are omitted.

Please permit a short personal experience. Once I served as trumpet soloist at the First Baptist Church of Jacksonville, Florida, accompanied by Camp Kirkland's church orchestra. The next morning, after taking my seat on a Delta jet, I was gleefully, but innocently, obstinate in sharing my liturgical overflow with the man sitting next to me. After proclaiming all my orchestral worship superlatives, I asked him what he did for a living. "I

serve as pastor of the _____Church of Christ,"
he grinned. Then emerged smiles of sheer
amazement! How could this be? How could the
two of us, with diametrically opposed views of
church instrumental music, be thrown together on
this particular weekend and have the opportunity to
exchange enjoyable pleasantries all the way to
Atlanta? He remained unconverted. So did I!

Yes, certain Christians persist in denying any
kind of instruments into their New Testament
churches. Dr. Hedrick gives a rather persuasive
scriptural accounting, meant not so much to rebuke
his detractors, but to lend sanctified credence to the
passions of his many friends.

These writings should increase the
understanding of instrumentalists as to how their
skillful performance brings honor to the Kingdom,
but Dr. Hedrick goes a step further: he provides
scripturally-based meditations, one for each
"pillar," to be used as devotionals in actual
rehearsals. In so doing, he lends stature to the
instruments and encourages those who play them
toward a meaningful relationship with God, whose
worship demands the best of their artistry, both
instrumental and spiritual.

Dr. G. Douglas Smith
Professor of Church Music
Southern Baptist Theological Seminary

iv

Chapter 1
Introduction

The Prevalence of Instrumental Music in Christian Worship

According to a National Congregations Study, published in the Journal for Scientific Study of Religion in 1999, 83% of religious congregations in the United States use a "musical instrument of any sort" as an element of their worship services. This high percentage is only exceeded by two other elements in this study: singing by the congregation (96%) and sermon or speech (95%).[1] The prevalent inclusion of instrumental music in worship, second only to singing and preaching in churches around the country, is indicative of the relative importance

---

[1]Mark Chaves, Mary Ellen Konieczny, Kraig Beyerlein, and Emily Barman, "The National Congregations Study: background, methods, and selected results," *Journal for the Scientific Study of Religion* 38, no. 4 (1999): 472.

of this element in the average Christian congregation. Churches across our nation are using instruments as a vital part of their weekly services, from a single piano, organ, or guitar, to a full orchestra or band.

The importance of instrumental music in Christian worship is firmly rooted in the history of our nation, from its very inception. Both A. Joseph King and Don Hustad recognize two groups as important precursors to the dominant presence of instrumental music in American church worship.[2] These two groups are the Moravians, beginning in the mid-1700s, and the Salvation Army, from the late 1800s.

Relevant Historical Practice of Instrumental Music in Worship

The Moravians

The Moravian church was first organized as the "Unity of the Brethren" in 1457, and for the first two centuries, existed mainly in Bohemia, Moravia, and Poland.[3] In 1735, the Moravian Church sent

---

[2]A. Joseph King, "Instrumental Music in Southern Baptist Life," *Baptist History and Heritage* 19.1 (January 1984): 48. Donald P. Hustad, *Jubilate II: Church Music in Worship and Renewal* (Carol Stream, IL: Hope Publishing Company, 1993), 506-507.

[3]Moravian Music Foundation, "The Moravian Church," http://www.moravianmusic.org/MMchurch.html (accessed August 10, 2007).

missionaries from Saxony to America, settling first in Savannah, Georgia,[4] then establishing a permanent settlement in Bethlehem, Pennsylvania.[5] They also established two other settlements in Pennsylvania, and three settlements in North Carolina, with Salem (now Winston-Salem) as their governing center.[6]

Moravian clergy and laypeople in Europe were well trained in classical music, and came to America with their instruments and a tradition of using them consistently in worship.[7] This tradition expressed itself in the form of orchestral and chamber music, as well as accompaniments for vocal solos and choir anthems for worship.[8] "Indeed, the phenomenal musical record of the early American Moravians is distinguished by the cultivation of instrumental music."[9]

In the infancy of the United States of America,

---

[4]Harry Hobart Hall, "The Moravian Wind Ensemble: Distinctive Chapter in America's History" (Ph.D. diss., George Peabody College for Teachers, 1967), iii.

[5]Moravian Music Foundation, "The Moravian Church."

[6]Hall, Ph.D. diss., iii.

[7]Moravian Music Foundation, "Moravian Music," http://www.moravianmusic.org/MMchurch.html (accessed August 10, 2007).

[8]Ibid.

[9]Hall, Ph.D. diss., 79.

instrumental music flourished under the influence of the Moravians. "During the first years of the young republic, the most and best music-making in America was not enjoyed in typical concert halls, but rather in the normal community and worship life of the Moravian band."[10] So we see that an excellent tradition of instrumental music in worship was established from the very inception of our nation.

The Salvation Army

William Booth founded the Salvation Army in 1865 in London, England.[11] Initially called the East London Christian Mission, this evangelistic street ministry expanded quickly and in 1878 adopted the title Salvation Army.[12] The open air evangelistic work was subject to quite a bit of opposition, not only from those opposed to the Gospel, but also from other Christians, who took exception to the Salvation Army's methods.[13] In 1878 therefore, the

---

[10]Hustad, *Jubilate II,* 214-215.

[11]Richard Collier, *The General Next to God: The Story of William Booth and the Salvation Army* (New York: E. P. Dutton and Co., Inc., 1965), 285.

[12]Peter Bale, "Brass Bands and the Salvation Army," *Brass-Forum.co.uk,* http://www.brass-forum.co.uk/Articles/BrassBandsintheSalvationArmy.htm (accessed August 10, 2007).

[13]Ibid.

Salvation Army secured the services of the Fry family as bodyguards and to help with crowd control. Charles Fry and his three sons also played brass instruments and were soon asked to play their instruments to assist with the singing in the streets. Thus, the first Salvation Army Band was formed, consisting of two cornets, a valve trombone, and a euphonium.[14]

The following year, Salvation Army corps bands began to be formed and organized, drawing the attention of founder, William Booth. In 1880, Booth encouraged the widespread development of bands to assist in the Salvation Army efforts, and in 1882, the Salvation Army began to publish their own brass arrangements.[15]

As the Salvation Army moved overseas, one of the first destinations was the United States, and along with that effort came the Salvation Army band movement. The first American corps bands were established in 1884 in East Liverpool, Ohio and Grand Rapids, Michigan.[16] Salvation Army bands multiplied quickly throughout the country, so that by 1941, *Newsweek* magazine reported that there were approximately 1000 corps bands in the United States, most with eight to fourteen

---

[14]Ronald W. Holz, *Brass Bands of the Salvation Army: Their Mission and Music* (Hitchin, England: 2006), 65.

[15]Ibid, 170.

[16]Ibid, 389.

members.[17] "The most typical and most numerous Salvation Army brass band is found at the local worship centre level, what for years has been called the Corps, later Corps Community centre, and more recently in some portions of the world, Community Worship and Service centre."[18]

John Philip Sousa, who was commissioned to write *The Salvation Army March* for the fiftieth anniversary of the Salvation Army in the United States, wrote the following commendation of Salvation Army bands in his article, "Why the World Needs Bands":

> If you want to know one of the very good reasons why the world needs bands just ask one of The Salvation Army warriors, who for years has marched carrying the cross through the back alleys of life. Let him tell of the armies of men that have been turned toward a better life by first hearing the sounds of a Salvation Army band. The next time you hear a Salvation Army band, no matter how humble, take off your hat.[19]

Both the Moravians and the Salvation Army

---

[17]Ibid.

[18]Ibid, 29.

[19]John Philip Sousa, "Why the World Needs Bands," *Etude Magazine* (September 1930), 48, cited in Holz, *Brass Bands of the Salvation Army,* 377.

helped to establish an early tradition of instrumental music in American Christian worship, which is exemplified dramatically today by the churches of the Southern Baptist Convention.

The Southern Baptist Convention

The Southern Baptist Convention is the largest Protestant denomination, according to a 2007 study by the Hartford Institute for Religion Research.[20] Southern Baptist churches have also been leaders in the contemporary movement towards the use of full orchestras in Christian worship. This phenomenon began in the mid-1970s and has grown and spread to other denominations across the country.

Camp Kirkland holds the distinction of being the first full-time director of instrumental music at a Southern Baptist church, when he assumed that position at First Baptist Church, Jacksonville, Florida, in July 1976.[21] Several other individuals followed Kirkland into full-time positions within a year: George Rawlin at First Baptist Church, Atlanta, Georgia, in November 1976 and Charles Krause at First Baptist Church, Roanoke, Virginia,

---

[20]Hartford Institute for Religion Research/Hartford Seminary (http://hirr.hartsem.edu/research/fastfacts/fast_facts.html#largest).

[21]Lawrence William Mayo, "Full-time Programs of Instrumental Music in Nine Selected Southern Baptist Churches." (DMA diss., Southern Baptist Theological Seminary, 1986), 6.

in June 1977.[22] In addition, Dr. G. Douglas Smith was hired at Southern Baptist Theological Seminary in 1975, with primary duties in instrumental music, and Dr. A. Joseph King began an instrumental music program at Southwestern Baptist Theological Seminary in 1978.[23] Finally, during that same time period, Gerald Armstrong, a former band director and minister of music, was hired as instrumental consultant for the Church Music Department of the Southern Baptist Convention (SBC) Sunday School Board.[24]

Even before the decade of 1970, Southern Baptists had a rich history of using instruments in worship. A 1939 survey of Southern Baptist churches showed 1700 churches maintaining some type of church orchestra.[25] Another indicator of the abundance of instrumental groups in Southern Baptist churches in the first half of the twentieth century was the sales of orchestrated hymnals, which totaled over 10,000 for Broadman Press, the publishing arm of the SBC.[26]

---

[22]King, "Instrumental Music in Southern Baptist Life," 52.

[23]A. Joseph King, "Praise the Lord with the Sound of the Trumpet," *The Church Musician,* October 1982, 5.

[24]Ibid.

[25]W. Hines Sims, *Instrumental Music in the Church* (Nashville, TN: Sunday School Board of the Southern Baptist Convention, 1947), 71.

[26]King, "Instrumental Music in Southern Baptist Life," 50.

Several factors contributed to the decline of these instrumental ensembles around the time of World War II, including the war itself, the rapid growth of music education programs in the public schools, and the rise of the graded choir program in churches around the country.[27] These factors led to a decade of relative inactivity, but after that time, instrumental groups began to reappear and grow under the influence of denominational leaders such as W. Hines Sims, a former band director and then secretary for the Sunday School Board of the SBC.[28] A 1968 survey of approximately 2000 churches with over 1000 members showed 409 with functioning instrumental ensembles, and of those, 22.5% with eleven to fifteen members, and most of the rest under eleven members.[29]

This rich history of instrumental music in Southern Baptist Convention churches, and the development of full orchestras in those churches during the decade of the 1970s, prompted the formation of an annual conference of church instrumental directors, for the purpose of sharing ideas, encouragement, and fellowship: the Metro Instrumental Directors Conference.

---

[27]Ibid.

[28]Ibid, 51.

[29]Ibid.

The Metro Instrumental Directors Conference

The Metro Instrumental Directors Conference (MIDC) was founded by Camp Kirkland in 1980. Kirkland had served as the instrumental music director at First Baptist Church, Jacksonville, Florida, since 1976,[30] and was encouraged by his Minister of Music to form the conference,[31] based on the model of the Music Metro Conference (for Ministers of Music), which was initiated in 1966.[32] The attendance at that first meeting, at First Baptist Church, Jacksonville, in May of 1980, consisted of seven church instrumental directors, a seminary professor, and a denominational worker.[33] Other churches represented at that initial meeting included Castle Hills First Baptist Church, San Antonio, Texas; First Baptist Church, Atlanta, Georgia; First Baptist Church, Dallas, Texas; First Baptist Church, Roanoke, Virginia; and North Phoenix Baptist Church, Phoenix, Arizona.[34]

---

[30] Mayo, DMA diss., 5-6.

[31] Camp Kirkland, interview by author, 11 September 2007, email.

[32] Mayo, Appendix F of DMA diss., 239-240.

[33] Steve Dunn, "Praise Him With… Instruments!" *Creator: The Bimonthly Magazine of Balanced Music Ministries,* September/October 2001, 4.

[34] David Winkler, interview by author, 17 August 2007, telephone.

The MIDC meets annually, usually in early May, and is hosted by one or more of the members from the previous conferences. The early meetings of the MIDC were informal gatherings, which were largely round-table discussions.[35] Other conference elements added over the years include reading sessions, with the directors bringing their instruments and playing new arrangements for church instrumental groups, and arranging contests, when participants would submit their own arrangements for church orchestra.

From the early days of the MIDC, even though the majority of directors in attendance have been from Southern Baptist churches, directors from churches outside the Southern Baptist Convention have been welcome. At one of the earliest meetings, in 1983 at First Baptist Church, Dallas, the instrumental director from First Assembly of God in Lakeland, Florida was invited to attend.[36] This inclusiveness stands in contrast to the membership qualifications of the MIDC's parent organization, the Metro Music Conference, which is for full-time Ministers of Music in Southern Baptist churches.[37]

---

[35]David Winkler, "Remembrances of the Early Metro Conferences," *25th Anniversary Metro Instrumental Directors Conference Notebook* (Cruise to Miami, Key West, and Cozumel: May 3-7, 2004).

[36]Steve Kirby, interview by author, 23 August 2007, email.

[37]Metro Music Conference, "Requirements and Invitation Procedures," adopted 12 February 1986, and "Metro I Membership Qualifications," approved at the 1997 Metro I Conference, Dallas, TX.

An early meeting, in 1981 at North Phoenix Baptist Church, ended with the group drafting a letter to major publishers, encouraging them to publish more music for church instrumental groups, with the needs of amateur musicians in mind.[38] Publishers responded and there was an explosion of new music published in the next two decades. Participants at the 1988 meeting at First Baptist Church in Carrolton, Texas, addressed the literature issue again with the publishers, in the form of a resolution. The issue at that point was not the volume of literature, but difficulty and accessibility of the parts for predominantly amateur players. Many of the major publishers responded with appropriate guidelines for their arrangers and orchestrators.

The growth in the amount of music available for church instrumental groups was also indicative of the growth in the number of directors attending the MIDC each year. The annual attendance steadily grew through the 1980s and into the 1990s. In 1993, a committee was formed to discuss the future of the MIDC, and specifically whether or not to place a limit on the number of attendees each year.[39] At the May 1995 meeting in Atlanta, Georgia, the committee issued the following statement:

---

[38]Winkler, "Remembrances of the Early Metro Conferences."

[39]Metro Instrumental Directors Conference, "MIDC Adopts Mission Statement," *Bulletin Board* Opus 1, No. 1 (June 1995): 1.

The Metro Instrumental Directors Conference exists to glorify God through providing a forum for encouragement, fellowship, and ministry growth to full-time church music associates who have primary responsibility in instrumental music, through an annual conference of the members, and other methods of communication throughout the year. The annual conference will be limited to the first sixty paid registrants. Respectfully submitted, May 4, 1995.[40]

Ever since this statement was adopted by the MIDC, attendance has fairly consistently hit the sixty-director limit, with as many as ninety-eight total participants at the 2000 meeting in Orlando, including thirty-three spouses and five vendors.[41] A recent meeting in Atlanta on May 15-18, 2007 had fifty-six directors in attendance, along with 28 spouses.[42]

Even though musical issues and the desire for Christian fellowship among like-minded church servants have dominated the agenda of the Metro Instrumental Directors Conference, there is also a profound appreciation among the group for God's word and its application to life and ministry. These instrumental directors, and others across the country, would benefit from a focused, detailed document that establishes the biblical foundations

---

[40]Ibid.

[41]Steve Kirby, interview by author, 21 August 2007, email.

[42]Jeff Cranfill, interview by author, 21 August 2007, email.

of instrumental music in worship.

The Purpose and the Problem

The purpose of this book is to provide an accessible, comprehensive biblical philosophy of instrumental music in worship for church instrumental directors and instrumentalists in churches. This information will better inform and enrich their ministry, transforming them as worship leaders, and ultimately, transforming the worship practices of their churches. This book will prove to be a valuable resource for directors, as they justify their ministry in their respective churches, but also as an apologetic to those from churches and denominations who refute the use of instrumental music in New Testament worship. Furthermore, this resource will provide a biblical basis for the practice of instrumental music ministry, beyond a simple justification, examining the scriptural guidelines for the ministry and operation of instrumental music in the worship of the church. This information is formatted in the appendix as a series of devotionals,[43] so directors are able to present it to their instrumental groups, making sure both directors and instrumentalists understand the biblical basis and guidelines for their practice of instrumental music in Christian worship. As the director presents this devotional series to his instrumentalists, he will more effectively internalize the biblical principles of the series, as he is required

---

[43]See appendix 3 for four-part devotional series.

to study the material and then verbalize it to his group.

A biblical understanding of the use of instrumental music in worship is of utmost importance to practicing church instrumentalists and directors. My concern is the fact that a well-defined, comprehensive biblical philosophy on this subject has not been readily available for church instrumental directors. When church instrumental directors are asked to justify their ministry from a biblical perspective, they have had relatively few resources to consult. I have discovered no books dedicated exclusively to the subject, and only two books with a complete chapter devoted to the biblical foundations of instrumental music in worship.[44] On the other hand, there is an abundance of written material readily available concerning the prohibition of instrumental music in worship. Individuals and denominations that generate this material take a position based solely on the regulative principle, otherwise know as the negative hermeneutic. "The 'negative hermeneutic' says that because something is not found in the New Testament," in this case, instrumental music, "it is

---

[44]Jon Duncan, "Biblical Foundations for Instrumental Music Ministry," in *The Instrumental Resource for Church and School,* ed. Julie Barrier and Jim Hansford (Nashville, TN: Church Street Press, 2002), 13-25, and Paul S. Jones, "A Biblical Case for Instruments in Worship," in *Singing and Making Music: Issues in Church Music Today* (Phillipsburg, NJ: P&R Publishing, 2006), 23-31.

inherently wrong and unbiblical."[45] I believe this position is unfounded, and needs to be addressed with a strong, comprehensive rationale for the use of instrumental music in Christian worship.

As I examined the biblical references to instrumental music in worship, I have organized the references into four basic pillars. The first pillar is the many references to instrumental music in the Psalms, which is related to the second pillar, the Davidic tradition of instrumental music in worship. King David is associated with many of the psalms, and was in large part responsible for establishing a tradition of instrumental music in ancient Hebrew worship that extended to Temple worship in Jesus' time.

The overwhelming majority of biblical references to instrumental music in worship are found in the Old Testament, but there are also limited references in the New Testament. The third pillar is the implied references in two familiar worship passages, Ephesians 5:19 and Colossians 3:16, and their reference to using psalms in Christian worship. I will also consider the reference to "making melody" in Ephesians 5:19, which is from the Greek word *psallo*, and has a possible connection to instrumental music. Finally, the fourth pillar is the mention of instruments in the context of heavenly worship in the book of Revelation.

---

[45]Rex A. Koivisto, *One Lord, One Faith* (Wheaton, IL: Victor Books, 1993), 169.

Chapter 2

Pillar One

The Psalms

The book of Psalms is rich with references to the use of musical instruments in worship of almighty God, and this pillar is the first in the biblical foundations for the use of instrumental music in worship. There are references in the text of fifteen different chapters, beginning in Psalm 33 and ending with half the verses in Psalm 150 (Psalm 33:2-3, 43:4, 45:8, 47:5, 57:8, 68:25, 71:22, 81:2-3, 92:3, 98:5-6, 108:2, 144:9, 147:7, 149:3, 150:3-5). An additional nine psalms mention instruments in the ascription or psalm heading (Psalm 4, 5, 6, 12, 54, 55, 61, 67, 76). All of these ascriptions prescribe instruments to accompany the reading or singing of the psalm. Therefore, a total of twenty-four of the one hundred and fifty psalms mention instruments, either to accompany the psalm or in the context of worship.[1]

Even though the instruments in the Psalms represent an ancient culture,[2] the variety reflected is amazing. All four families of musical instruments are represented: woodwinds, brass, percussion, and strings. No kind of instrument is excluded! Psalm 150 is representative of this diversity with its mention of the pipe, trumpet, timbrel, cymbals, harp, lyre, and stringed instruments.[3] As R. C. Sproul so eloquently puts it, "Psalm 150 indicates virtually all of the elements of orchestral music are present and sanctioned by God for worship."[4]

Praise Him with *trumpet* sound;
Praise Him with *harp* and *lyre*.
Praise Him with *timbrel* and dancing;
Praise Him with *stringed instruments* and *pipe*.
Praise Him with *loud cymbals*
Praise Him with *resounding cymbals*.
(Psalm 150:3-5, emphasis mine)

---

[1]See Appendix 2 for texts to the twenty-four references.

[2]The oldest psalms date before the monarchy (1050 B.C.), and the Book of Psalms, as we know it, was probably not complete until the fourth century B.C. Peter C. Craigie, *Psalms 1-50* in *Word Biblical Commentary* (Waco, TX: Word Books, 1983), 31.

[3]Psalm 150:3-5 (All Biblical references are taken from the New American Standard Bible, unless otherwise mentioned).

[4]R. C. Sproul, *A Taste of Heaven: Worship in the Light of Eternity* (Lake Mary, FL: Reformation Trust Publishing, 2006), 153.

Of particular interest is the fact that, although dance accompanies the listing of instruments in Psalm 150, singing is not mentioned. This exclusion would indicate that instrumental music, by itself, could be considered an act of praise. According to John Frame, "In Psalm 150, the instruments do not merely accompany praise; in my view, they are means of praise."[5] Barry Liesch suggests that there are other psalms (Ps. 43:4 and 147:7) that seem "to support the idea of instrumental praise in and of itself... without the necessity of accompanying words."[6]

Not only is the variety of instruments listed in the Psalms inclusive, but also the kind of individuals that typically played them. The priests usually played the trumpets (1 Chron. 15:24, Neh. 12:41), while Levites are described as playing the lyre, harp and cymbals (1 Chron. 25:1, 6, Neh. 12:27). Women typically played other instruments, like the timbrel, or tambourine, as they danced (Ps. 68:25). As Bible commentator A.F. Kirkpatrick notes, "Thus the call to praise is addressed to priests, Levites, and people; and every kind of

---

[5]John M. Frame, *Worship in Spirit and Truth* (Phillipsburg, NJ: Presbyterian and Reformed Publishing Company, 1996), 130.

[6]Barry Liesch, *People in the Presence of God: Models and Directions for Worship* (Grand Rapids: Zondervan Publishing House, 1988), 193.

instrument is to be enlisted in the service."[7]

The context of worship in the fifteen textual references in the Psalms is understood from their undeniable association with the worship attitudes of joy, praise, and thanksgiving. Psalm 33 is representative of this association:

> *Sing for joy* in the Lord, O you righteous ones;
> *Praise* is becoming to the upright.
> *Give thanks* to the Lord with the lyre;
> *Sing praises* to Him with a harp of ten strings.
> Sing to Him a new song;
> Play skillfully *with a shout of joy*.
> (Psalm 33:1-3, emphasis mine)

With only the harp and the lyre mentioned, there is not quite the diversity of instruments in this psalm as in Psalm 150, but biblical commentator Peter C. Craigie suggests, "no doubt these two instruments merely symbolize the entire array of instruments in the orchestra that would be utilized in the accompaniment of praise."[8]

The special emphases in verse 3 of Psalm 33 should also be noted. In addition to the directive to "play skillfully," we are also encouraged to praise God with "a new song." Derek Kidner says we

---

[7]A. F. Kirkpatrick, *The Book of Psalms* in *The Cambridge Bible for Schools and Colleges* (Cambridge: Cambridge University Press, 1921), 832.

[8]Peter C. Craigie, *Psalms 1-50* in *Word Biblical Commentary* (Waco, TX: Word Books, 1983), 272.

should, "Note the call for freshness and skill as well as fervour: three qualities rarely found together in religious music."[9] This emphasis on ministry with excellence is also reflected in Charles Spurgeon's comments on this verse: "It is wretched to hear God praised in a slovenly manner. He deserves the best that we have."[10]

The psalms were composed for use in the temple service, and the Psalter was basically the temple songbook.[11] This designation is supported by the information in many of the psalm ascriptions, and from the Rabbinic traditions in the Mishnah and the Talmud.[12] Donald Hustad calls the Psalms "the hymnal of Israel,"[13] pointing out that "the psalms were sung in regular sequence following the morning sacrifices on specified days of the week and were accompanied by instruments."[14] In

---

[9]Derek Kidner, *Psalms 1-72* in *The Tyndale Old Testament Commentaries* (London: Inter-Varsity Press, 1973), 136.

[10]Charles H. Spurgeon, *The Treasury of David,* Vol. 1, *Psalm 1-57* (Peabody, MA: Hendrickson Publishers, 1988), 105.

[11]Sigmund Mowinckel, *The Psalms in Israel's Worship,* Vol. 2 (Grand Rapids: William B. Eerdmans Publishing Company, 2004), 202.

[12]Ibid.

[13]Donald P. Hustad, *Jubilate II: Church Music in Worship and Renewal* (Carol Stream, IL: Hope Publishing Company, 1993), 137.

[14]Ibid.

addition, they may have been interrupted with an instrumental interlude, possibly indicated by the word *Selah.* This word is found seventy-one times in the text of thirty-nine Psalms, and even though the meaning is relatively obscure, Andrew Hill acknowledges that it may suggest "a pause for a musical interlude."[15] Richard C. Leonard agrees that *Selah* "is most often interpreted to indicate an instrumental interlude."[16]

Alfred Sendrey writes in support of the translation of *Selah* as an instrumental interlude: "The simplest explanation of the term, generally considered authentic, is hinted at by the Talmudic tradition:[17]

> Ben Azra clashed the cymbal and the Levites broke forth into singing. When they reached a break in the singing, they (the priests) blew the trumpets and the people prostrated themselves; at every break there was a blowing of the trumpets and at every blowing of the trumpet a prostration" (Mishnah, Tal. Bab., Erubin 54a).

---

[15] Andrew E. Hill, *Baker's Handbook of Bible Lists* (Grand Rapids: Baker Books, 1981), 200.

[16] Richard C. Leonard, "Psalms in Biblical Worship," in *The Biblical Foundations of Christian Worship,* ed. Robert E. Webber, vol. 1, *The Complete Library of Christian Worship* (Nashville: Star Song, 1993), 244.

[17] Alfred Sendrey, *Music in the Social and Religious Life of Antiquity* (Cranbury, NJ: Associated University Presses, Inc., 1974), 132.

This quote, referenced by Sendrey, was part of the Mishnah, which is the written version of the traditional Jewish oral law. Even though it refers to Temple worship, David greatly influenced Temple worship practice, and therefore it sheds great light on the probable meaning of *Selah*.

Dismissing the possible connection of *Selah* to instrumental music, we have still established that twenty-four psalms reference praising God with instruments, and the psalms were used as the songbook of Israel. Does it not then demand the accompaniment of those psalms with instruments? As Paul Jones points out, "it is less likely that we fully benefit from the psalm without the reality of their presence. And it is, at the least, strange to sing the words 'Praise the LORD with trumpets and cymbals' without any instruments to demonstrate or authenticate that which is being sung."[18]

---

[18]Paul S. Jones, *Singing and Making Music: Issues in Church Music Today* (Phillipsburg, NJ: Presbyterian and Reformed Publishing Company, 2006), 27.

Chapter 3
Pillar Two
Davidic Worship

Closely related to instrumental music in the book of Psalms is the use of instruments in Davidic worship, which is the second pillar in the biblical foundations for the use of instrumental music in worship. King David was known as the sweet psalmist of Israel (2 Sam. 23:1). In the psalm headings or ascriptions, David is the individual most frequently mentioned. Even though this frequency might indicate other things,[1] Craigie admits, "The probability remains...that a number of the psalms in the Psalter which are associated with David may be Davidic

---

[1] For the use of David, belonging to David, or dedicated to David. Peter C. Craigie, *Psalms 1-50* in *Word Biblical Commentary* (Waco, TX: Word Books, 1983), 34-35.

compositions."[2] David is also largely responsible for the Old Testament tradition of instrumental music in worship, which began as he ascended the throne of Israel, and extended to the time of Christ.

Prior to the reign of King David, musical instruments were practically nonexistent in the formal worship of Israel. Except for one isolated passage in the book of Numbers,[3] worship in the tabernacle before David was seemingly devoid of any music, and in the giving of the Law on Mount Sinai, there were no commandments regarding the use of instruments as part of the tabernacle ritual.[4] In fact, Peter Leithart says, "So far as we can tell from the information in the Pentateuch, this ritual was performed in silence."[5]

In this passage, from 1 Chronicles 16, after David brought the Ark of the Covenant into Jerusalem and pitched a tent for it there, we see the inception of instrumental music in Israel's worship ritual:

---

[2]Ibid, 35.

[3]Num. 10:10 - "Also in the day of your gladness and in your appointed feasts, and on the first days of your months, you shall blow the trumpets over your burnt offerings, and over the sacrifices of your peace offerings; and they shall be as a reminder of you before your God. I am the Lord your God."

[4]David W. Music, *With Stringed Instruments...Or Not?* (Internet article: www.lifeway.com, July 18, 2005), 1.

[5]Peter J. Leithart, *From Silence to Song: The Davidic Liturgical Revolution* (Moscow, ID: Canon Press, 2003), 54.

And he appointed some of the Levites as ministers before the ark of the Lord, even to celebrate and to thank and praise the Lord God of Israel: Asaph the chief, and second to him Zechariah, then Jeiel, Shemiramoth, Jehiel, Mattithiah, Eliab, Benaiah, Obed-edom, and Jeiel, with musical instruments, harps, lyres; also Asaph played loud-sounding cymbals, and Benaiah and Jahaziel the priests blew trumpets continually before the ark of the covenant of God. Then on that day David first assigned Asaph and his relatives to give thanks to the Lord (1 Chron. 16:4-7).

In commenting on these verses, Jeremy Montagu notes that "King David establishes what we presume to have become the permanent, or at least the regular Temple orchestra, a rather small band of eight string players, two trumpeters, and one cymbal player."[6] Later, in 1 Chronicles 23:5, the Levitical orchestra seems to grow to four thousand, a figure that Montagu thinks is an exaggeration by the writer of Chronicles,[7] but is none-the-less indicative of the importance of instrumental music in worship to King David. Other commentators feel that the Hebrew word, translated "thousand," is more accurately understood as a clan

---

[6]Jeremy Montagu, *Musical Instruments of the Bible* (Lanham, MD: Scarecrow Press, 2002), 63.

[7]Ibid.

or group.[8] Perhaps a more reasonable orchestra of twenty-five players is mentioned later in 1 Chronicles 25:1-6.

Even though instrumental music was largely absent from worship throughout the history of the Tabernacle of Moses, David chose to add instruments to their ritual in Gibeon, after he established his own tabernacle in Jerusalem:

> And he left Zadok the priest and his relatives the priests before the tabernacle of the Lord in the high place which was at Gibeon, to offer burnt offerings to the Lord on the altar of burnt offering continually morning and evening, even according to all that is written in the law of the Lord, which He commanded Israel. And with them were Heman and Jeduthun, and the rest who were chosen, who were designated by name, to give thanks to the Lord, because His lovingkindness is everlasting. And with them were Heman and Jeduthun with trumpets and cymbals for those who should sound aloud, and with instruments for the songs of God, and the sons of Jeduthun for the gate (1 Chron. 16:39-42).

So we have two tabernacles existing at the same time, one on Mt. Gibeon and one on Mt. Zion (Jerusalem), only the one in Jerusalem containing the Ark of the Covenant, but both with musical

---

[8]Andrew E. Hill, *1 & 2 Chronicles* in *The NIV Application Commentary* (Grand Rapids: Zondervan, 2003), 302.

instruments used in praise and worship of God.

Under Moses, one of the primary duties of the Levites was the care and transportation of the wilderness tabernacle and all its furnishings (Num. 3:5-8 and Deut. 10:8). Now that the tent housing the Ark of the Covenant was in its final resting place, the job description of the Levites changed dramatically. The Levites were no longer the moving crew for the Tabernacle. Instead, David set about training them to sing and play instruments, and then set them apart for the service of the Lord through music:

> Moreover, David and the commanders of the army set apart for the service some of the sons of Asaph and of Heman and of Jeduthun, who were to prophesy with lyres, harps, and cymbals; All these were under the direction of their father to sing in the house of the Lord, with cymbals, harps and lyres, for the service of the house of God. Asaph, Jeduthun and Heman were under the direction of the king. And their number who were trained in singing to the Lord, with their relatives, all who were skillful, was 288. And they cast lots for their duties, all alike, the small as well as the great, the teacher as well as the pupil (1 Chron. 25:1, 6-8).

Curt Sachs makes the following comment on these verses:

> The musical scene was completely altered in the days of David and Solomon... At that time,

Israel began to develop professional musicians and a musical organization. David bade the head of the Levites to train musicians who were to sing and play when the Ark of the Covenant was carried into Jerusalem. But when he made preparations for the Temple, no less than two hundred and eighty-eight Levites became students of an actual academy of ritual music and, divided into twenty-four groups, were taught by their fathers for song in the house of the Lord, with cymbals, harps, and lyres.[9]

Old Testament scholar Andrew Hill believes that the formation of these professional music guilds was King David's most significant contribution to the practice of Hebrew religion.[10] 1 Chronicles 23:5 even includes a reference to "the instruments which David made for giving praise." These musical instruments, associated with Davidic worship in the Old Testament, reflect all four families: woodwinds, brass, percussion and strings. Let's examine these instruments and how were they used in the worship of ancient Israel.

The *ugab* is a woodwind instrument, but its exact identity has been a matter of considerable

---

[9]Curt Sachs, "Music in the Bible," in *The Universal Jewish Encyclopedia* (1942).

[10]Andrew E. Hill, *Enter His Courts With Praise!* (Grand Rapids: Baker Books, 1996), 40.

debate.[11] It is mentioned four times in the Old Testament (Gen. 4:21, Ps. 150:4, Job 21:12, 30:31), but only one of those references can be associated with Davidic worship: Psalm 150:4. According to Joachim Braun, Curt Sachs offers the only plausible explanation of what this instrument really was, which is a kind of long flute.[12] Both the NIV and NLT translations of the Bible identify this instrument as a flute, while the NASB translates it as a pipe, which would also be accurate. Unfortunately, the KJV translated it as an organ, which realistically was not an instrument that was in existence at the time.

The *hazozerah* is a brass instrument and has the distinction of being the only instrument that the Old Testament provides detailed information about. It was a trumpet, made of beaten or hammered silver, with a long narrow body and a flared bell.[13] It is mentioned some eight times associated with Davidic style worship (1 Chron. 13:8, 15:24, 28, 16:6, 42; 2 Chron. 5:12-13, 29:26-28; Ps. 98:6), and was most often played by the priests. Montagu speculates that these straight trumpets were played by buzzing the lips in a mouthpiece, much like modern brass instruments, and that only three notes were possible, the lowest

---

[11]Joachim Braun, *Music in Ancient Palestine/Israel* (Grand Rapids: Eerdmans, 2002), 31.

[12]Braun, *Music in Ancient Palestine/Israel,* 32.

[13]Ibid, 15.

of which was really not functional.[14]

The *shophar* has the distinction of being the only wind instrument used in the worship of the Old Testament that is still currently found in modern worship, particularly Jewish worship. It is also the instrument that is mentioned most frequently in the Old Testament, seventy-four times, and is mentioned four times in association with Davidic worship (2 Sam. 6:15; 1 Chron 15:28; Ps. 98:6, 150:3). This instrument is commonly understood to be a ram's horn, and is played by buzzing the lips in the small end of the horn. Even though it is not made of brass, I have grouped it with the brass family, since it is played in a similar manner. Montagu points out that "because of the irregular bore... the overtones are seldom harmonic."[15]

The percussion instruments used in the Davidic worship tradition offer us the most variety, and all five of them are mentioned in one particular passage: 2 Samuel 6:5. The *seberosim* and *mena`an`im* are only mentioned in this one passage, and are identified as a clapper and a rattle respectively. The *meziltayim* is the most frequently mentioned percussion instrument in Davidic worship (2 Sam. 6:5; 1 Chron. 13:8, 15:16, 19, 28, 16:5, 42, 25:1, 6; 2 Chron. 5:12, 13, 29:25; Ezra 3:10; Neh. 12:27), and most scholars

---

[14]Montagu, *Musical Instruments of the Bible,* 128.

[15]Montagu, *Musical Instruments of the Bible,* 136.

agree that these were cymbals.[16] The *selselim* were also cymbals, but are mentioned much less frequently, in only 2 Samuel 6:5 and Psalm 150:5. As far as how these cymbals were played, Montagu believes that if they were large cymbals, they were struck face to face, like modern crash cymbals, but if they were smaller, they were struck edge to edge, like modern finger cymbals.[17] The final percussion instrument found in Davidic worship was the *toph*. This instrument is found in four different Davidic worship scriptures (2 Sam. 6:5; 1 Chron. 13:8; Ps. 149:3, 150:4), and resembled a modern tambourine, but without the metal jingles.[18] It was also played similar to a tambourine, being held with one hand, while struck with the hand or the fingers of the other hand.[19]

The *kinnor* and *nebhel* were both string instruments, and most likely lyres or small harps. The kinnor is the smaller of the two lyres and is traditionally associated with David, as the instrument he probably played.[20] It is also the instrument most frequently mentioned in Davidic worship, with 19 references (2 Sam. 6:5; 1 Chron. 13:8, 15:16, 21, 28, 16:5, 25:1, 3, 6; 2 Chron. 5:12,

---

[16]Braun, *Music in Ancient Palestine/Israel,* 20.

[17]Montagu, *Musical Instruments of the Bible,* 129-130.

[18]Braun, *Music in Ancient Palestine/Israel,* 30.

[19]Montagu, *Musical Instruments of the Bible,* 131.

[20]Braun, *Music in Ancient Palestine/Israel,* 17.

29:25; Ps. 33:2, 43:4, 71:22, 98:5, 147:7, 149:3, 150:3; Neh. 12:27). The nebhel is believed to have been slightly larger than the kinnor, and is mentioned almost as many times in association with Davidic worship (2 Sam. 6:5; 1 Chron 13:8, 15:16, 20, 28, 16:5, 25:1, 6; 2 Chron. 5:12, 29:25; Ps. 33:2, 71:22, 144:9, 150:3; Neh. 12:27). Montagu writes that both instruments were plucked with both hands, or possibly played with a plectrum or pick.[21] "Taking the Psalms as a whole," he says, "it is quite clear that the string instruments... are in the overwhelming majority. That the lyre, kinnor, should lead is, as King David's own instrument, appropriate enough. It was the most respected instrument of antiquity in general, not only of ancient Israel."[22]

After the reign of King David, periods of moral and spiritual revival in Israel's history often included a return to the worship practices of David and the use of musical instruments in worship. As Daniel Caram points out, "The revivalists always came back to the Davidic order of worship, not the Mosaic order."[23]   In 726 B.C., King Hezekiah repaired the house of the Lord and restored Davidic worship:

---

[21]Montagu, *Musical Instruments of the Bible,* 145.

[22]Ibid, 83.

[23]Daniel G. Caram, *Tabernacle of David* (Longwood, FL: Xulon Press, 2003), 98.

He then stationed the Levites in the house of the Lord with cymbals, with harps, and with lyres, *according to the command of David* and of Gad the king's seer, and of Nathan the prophet; for the command was from the Lord through His prophets. And the Levites stood *with the musical instruments of David*, and the priests with the trumpets. Then Hezekiah gave the order to offer the burnt offering on the altar. When the burnt offering began, the song to the Lord also began with the trumpets, *accompanied by the instruments of David, king of Israel*. While the whole assembly worshiped, the singers also sang and the trumpets sounded; all this continued until the burnt offering was finished (2 Chron. 29:25-28, emphasis mine).

After the restoration of Judah from Babylon in 536 B.C., the first order of business was to rebuild the Temple, and even before it was finished, Davidic worship with musical instruments was reinstituted:

Now when the builders had laid the foundation of the temple of the Lord, the priests stood in their apparel with trumpets, and the Levites, the sons of Asaph, with cymbals, to praise the Lord *according to the directions of King David of Israel* (Ezra 3:10, emphasis mine).

Finally, when Nehemiah was successful in rebuilding the walls of Jerusalem a number of years later, the dedication ceremony included a reference to two great choirs and musicians "with the musical instruments of David the man of God" (Neh. 12:36). Kevin Conner reminds us "that the godly Kings of Israel who brought Israel back to the Lord always restored the order of worship that was established by David the King in the Tabernacle of David."[24]

The ultimate goal of Christian worship is to give God glory and to seek his presence in our gatherings. God's manifest presence therefore, in response to instrumental music in worship, is a sign of his affirmation. This affirmation is most clearly demonstrated during the dedication of Solomon's Temple, with instruments in the Davidic tradition:

> And when the priests came forth from the holy place (for all the priests who were present had sanctified themselves, without regard to divisions), and all the Levitical singers, Asaph, Heman, Jeduthun, and their sons and kinsmen, clothed in fine linen, *with cymbals, harps, and lyres*, standing east of the altar, and with them *one hundred and twenty priests blowing trumpets* (2 Chron. 5:11-12, emphasis mine).

This impressive orchestra at the Temple dedication included cymbals, harps, and lyres, which were the traditional instruments in the Davidic tradition, but there were also one hundred

---

[24]Kevin J. Conner, *The Tabernacle of David* (Portland, OR: City Bible Publishing, 1989), 145.

and twenty trumpets. "Any time that 120 trumpeters are mentioned in the context of worship, instrumental music has to be seen as being of great importance for worship."[25] The huge number of trumpeters is attributed to the fact that there were twenty-four divisions of the priests, with five priests playing trumpet in each division. Therefore, all twenty-four divisions were involved in the dedication service.[26]

The Temple service reaches its climax when the instruments and singers are unified in praise of almighty God:

> In unison when the trumpeters and the singers were to make themselves heard with one voice to praise and to glorify the Lord, and when they lifted up their voice accompanied by *trumpets and cymbals and instruments of music*, and when they praised the Lord saying, "He indeed is good for His lovingkindness is everlasting," then the house, the house of the Lord, was filled with a cloud, so that the priests could not stand to minister because of the cloud, *for the glory of the Lord filled the house of God* (2 Chron. 5:13-14, emphasis mine).

---

[25]Charles E. Curl, "Developing a Theology of Worship to Inform the Use of Musical Instruments" (D.Min. dissertation, Drew University, 1961), 32.

[26]Sara Japhet, *I & II Chronicles: A Commentary* in *The Old Testament Library* (Louisville KY: Westminster/John Knox Press, 1993), 580.

This physical manifestation of God's presence was God's stamp of approval not only on the Temple, but also on the worship that accompanied the dedication, with musical instruments, in the Davidic tradition.

Chapter 4

Pillar Three

New Testament

Implied References

As we examine the Gospel accounts, the book of Acts, and the Epistles in the New Testament, it seems there are no obvious biblical references to the use of instruments in the worship of the early church. This apparent exclusion is primarily due to the infancy of the early church, its clandestine nature, and its relative lack of resources. There were many other reasons for this apparent void of musical instruments in early Christian worship, but those will be discussed in Chapter 7, under historical considerations.

Despite this perceived omission of instrumental music in the New Testament, two familiar New Testament worship passages suggest a link to the use of instruments in Christian worship. These two passages, Ephesians 5:19 and Colossians 3:16, comprise the third pillar of the biblical foundations for the use of instruments in worship. Both these passages reference the use of psalms, hymns, and spiritual songs in worship:

> Speaking to one another in psalms and hymns and spiritual songs, singing and making melody with your heart to the Lord; (Eph. 5:19)

> Let the word of Christ richly dwell within you, with all wisdom teaching and admonishing one another with psalms and hymns and spiritual songs, singing with thankfulness in your hearts to God. (Col. 3:16)

Noted biblical commentator Matthew Henry acknowledges that, "By psalms may be meant David's psalms, or such composures as were fitly sung with musical instruments."[1] This undeniable tie to pillar one, the Psalms, and correspondingly, musical instruments, alone justifies these references as the third pillar in the biblical foundations of instrumental music in worship.

The latter half of Ephesians 5:19, though, reveals yet another biblical support for the use of musical instruments in Christian worship: "singing and

---

[1]Matthew Henry, *Matthew Henry's Commentary on the Whole Bible,* Vol. 6, *Acts to Revelation* (McLean, VA: MacDonald Publishing Company, 1985), 713.

making melody with your heart to the Lord." John Stott writes that "singing and making melody" suggests that "perhaps the verbs combine vocal and instrumental music."[2] Even though these verses are often used to support the use of vocal music, and only vocal music, in Christian worship, there is the implied reference to the use of musical instruments, through the association with the Psalms, and also the fact that both vocalists and instrumentalists are able to "make melody" with their heart to the Lord.

Markus Barth, whose commentary on Ephesians is generally considered one of the best by most scholars,[3] translates Ephesians 5:19: "Talk to one another in psalms and hymns and spiritual songs. Sing *and play* to the Lord from your heart" (emphasis mine).[4] The Greek word, translated "making melody" in the NASB, and which Barth translates "play," is *psallo*. Barth maintains, "If… the original meaning of *psallo* is in mind, that is 'to pluck or twang a string' (in particular the bowstrings of a musical instrument), then 5:19 encourages the use of fiddles, harps, and other instruments."[5]

---

[2]John R. W. Stott, *The Message of Ephesians* in *The Bible Speaks Today* (Downers Grove, IL: Inter-Varsity Press, 1979), 206.

[3]David R. Bauer, *An Annotated Guide to Biblical Resources for Ministry* (Peabody, MA: Hendrickson Publishers, 2003), 276.

[4]Markus Barth, *Ephesians* in *The Anchor Bible* (New York: Doubleday & Company, Inc., 1974), 554-555.

[5]Ibid, 584.

Other writers confirm this interpretation of the word *psallo*,[6] but there is definitely not universal agreement among biblical scholars. Even Barth points out that Paul uses this same word in 1 Corinthians 14:15, but "The component of musical accompaniment has fully receded there."[7] Nevertheless, there is the allusion to the original meaning of *psallo,* which suggests the use of musical instruments.

Reading Colossians 3:16, in the context of the verses around it, reveals further support for the use of instruments to glorify God. After encouraging the Church at Colosse to "admonish one another with psalms and hymns and spiritual songs," the apostle Paul says, "And whatever you do in word or deed, do all in the name of the Lord Jesus, giving thanks through Him to God the Father" (Col. 3:17). *Whatever* you do, including playing an instrument, can and should be done in the name of the Lord Jesus.

Ephesians 5:19 and Colossians 3:16, therefore, contain an implied reference to the use of instrumental music in Christian worship, specifically through their reference to the use of

---

[6]Jon Duncan, "Biblical Foundations for Instrumental Music Ministry," in *The Instrumental Resource for Church and School,* ed. Julie Barrier and Jim Hansford (Nashville, TN: Church Street Press, 2002), 18. Harold W. Hoehner, *Ephesians: An Exegetical Commentary* (Grand Rapids: Baker Academic, 2002), 711.

[7]Markus Barth and Helmut Blanke, *Colossians* in *The Anchor Bible* (New York: Doubleday& Company, Inc., 1994), 428.

psalms, but the Ephesians passage may even include a direct command to praise the Lord with instruments, if we consider the literal meaning of the Greek word *psallo.*

Chapter 5
Pillar Four
The Book of Revelation

Instrumental music may or may not be directly referenced in the New Testament practices of the early church, depending on the understanding of the Greek word *psallo,* but what about the references to musical instruments in the heavenly worship of the Book of Revelation? In his book, *A Theology of Music for Worship Derived from the Book of Revelation,* Thomas Allen Seel maintains that "the Book of Revelation contains more instruments by name than the remainder of the New Testament."[1]

Harps are mentioned three times in Revelation, in 5:8, 14:2, and 15:2. This "harp (or lyre) was the

---

[1]Thomas Allen Seel, *A Theology of Music for Worship Derived From the Book of Revelation* (Metuchen, NJ: The Scarecrow Press, Inc., 1995), 85.

traditional instrument used in the singing of the Psalms"[2] (Psalm 33:2, 43:4, 57:8, 71:22, 81:2, 92:3, 98:5, 108:2, 144:9, 147:7, 149:3, 150:3). In fact, as commentator David Aune points out, the instrument commonly translated as harp or lyre is also the most frequently mentioned instrument in the Old Testament.[3]

Each of these references to harps in Revelation suggests many instruments, gathered before the victorious Lamb of God in heavenly worship:

> And when He had taken the book, the four living creatures and the twenty-four elders fell down before the Lamb, *having each one a harp,* and golden bowls full of incense, which are the prayers of the saints. (Rev. 5:8, emphasis mine)

> And I looked, and behold, the Lamb was standing on Mount Zion, and with Him one hundred and forty-four thousand, having His name and the name of His Father written on their foreheads. And I heard a voice from heaven, like the sound of many waters and like the sound of loud thunder, and the voice which I heard was like *the sound of harpists playing on*

---

[2]Robert H. Mounce, *The Book of Revelation* in *The New International Commentary on the New Testament* (Grand Rapids: William B. Eerdmans Publishing Company, 1977), 146.

[3]David E. Aune, *Revelation 1-5* in *Word Biblical Commentary* (Dallas: Word Books, 1997), 356.

their harps. (Rev. 14:1-2, emphasis mine)

And I saw, as it were, a sea of glass mixed with fire, and those who had come off victorious from the beast and from his image and from the number of his name, standing on the sea of glass, *holding harps of God*. And they sang the song of Moses the bond-servant of God and the song of the Lamb. (Rev. 15:2-3a, emphasis mine)

The other instrument mentioned repeatedly in the book of Revelation is the trumpet. The seven angels in Revelation 8 are given seven trumpets to sound, as "each one heralds the subsequent revelatory action in the text."[4] Although it may be debated whether or not these references are in the context of worship, Aune suggests that the use of the trumpet in Revelation is derived from Judaism.[5] The trumpet was used in ancient Israel and in early Judaism for a number of purposes, including praise of God, as was shown under pillar two (Davidic Worship). Seel sees a profound connection between the angelic use of trumpets in Revelation, and the priestly function of trumpets in the Old Testament: "Instrumental heralding (specifically, the trumpet call) is used to announce the revelation of the

---

[4]Seel, *Revelation,* 91.

[5]David E. Aune, *Revelation 6-16* in *Word Biblical Commentary* (Nashville: Thomas Nelson Publishers, 1998), 510.

Godhead. Only the angels, as agents of the Godhead, are called upon to play the trumpet. Used in a priestly context, trumpets are symbols of the Godhead."[6]

Seel contrasts this function of heralding, for trumpets, with the traditional function of the harps mentioned in Revelation, which is instrumental accompaniment of voices "used to aid in the vocal response to the Godhead."[7] Therefore, we see two distinct functions of the use of instrumental music in praise and worship of God, as represented in Revelation: heralding God's revelation and accompaniment of voices. These two functions point to the contemporary use of instruments in Christian worship, specifically the use of instrumental preludes and offertories, and the use of instruments to accompany choirs and congregational singing.

As instrumental groups prepare for their weekly worship services, they may rehearse music that falls into three general categories: congregational accompaniments, choral accompaniments, and instrumental features. Congregational and choral accompaniments reflect the traditional function of harps in the Book of Revelation, accompaniment of voices. Of the two, congregational accompaniment is the most important role of the instrumentalist, because it is the one thing that involves the entire church simultaneously in active participation.

---

[6]Seel, *Revelation,* 124.

[7]Ibid.

Instrumental features may take the form of preludes or offertories in the traditional Christian worship service. Even though this role is less important for the instrumentalist, as it only involves them actively, it fulfills the second function of instruments in the Book of Revelation, which is heralding God's revelation. If we consider the entire worship service God's revelation, then the prelude serves in that function. In many churches, the offertory is just before the sermon, so an instrumental piece in that spot also serves that function, heralding the revelation of God's word in the form of the sermon.

Even with the limited instrumentation indicated in Revelation, only harps and trumpets, the full spectrum of the functions of instrumental music in worship is reflected. There is also an indication that God is pleased with instrumental music in worship,[8] and if God is pleased with instrumental music in heavenly worship, would He not also be pleased with instruments in earthly worship? Our limited worship on earth is but preparation for our occupation in all eternity, and that should be reflective of the biblical model in Revelation, including the use of musical instruments.

---

[8]King, "Praise the Lord with the Sound of the Trumpet," *The Church Musician,* October 1982, 7.

Chapter 6
Theological Considerations

The primary theological factor when considering the subject of instrumental music in the Bible is the regulative principle, otherwise known as the negative hermeneutic. The regulative principle is terminology employed by Presbyterian and Reformed churches, and maintains, "whatever scripture does not command is forbidden," in other words, "Scripture must positively require a practice, if that practice is to be suitable for the worship of God."[1] This principle is very similar to the negative hermeneutic, which was terminology first used by Rex Koivisto, in his book, *One Lord, One Faith.*[2]

---

[1]John M. Frame, *Worship in Spirit and Truth* (Phillipsburg, NJ: Presbyterian and Reformed Publishing Company, 1996), 38.

[2]Rex A. Koivisto, *One Lord, One Faith* (Wheaton, IL: Victor Books, 1993), 169, cited in Aubrey Malphurs, *Doing Church: A Biblical Guide for Leading Ministries Through Change* (Grand Rapids: Kregal Publications, 1999), 71.

While the regulative principle seems to include all of scripture in its consideration of what is proper and what is not, Koivisto appears to consider only the New Testament in his definition of the negative hermeneutic.[3] Instrumental music is abundant in the Psalms and in Davidic worship, as we have shown in pillars one and two, so the regulative principle is not as relevant to our consideration as the more specific negative hermeneutic. The position embraced by several denominations, based on the negative hermeneutic, maintains that because instrumental music is not specifically mentioned in the worship of the New Testament church, we should not use it in Christian worship today.

Ignoring the previous discussion in pillars three and four, there are other reasons that the negative hermeneutic is inaccurate. Both Koivisto and Malphurs stress that just because something is not found in scripture, doesn't necessarily mean that it is prohibited.[4] "Absence of proof isn't proof of absence."[5] Malphurs also points out that it is extremely difficult to practice the negative hermeneutic consistently.[6] Where do we draw the line on what is acceptable and what is not? Are

---

[3]Koivisto, *One Lord, One Faith,* 169.

[4]Koivisto, *One Lord, One Faith,* 170; Malphurs, *Doing Church,* 66.

[5]Malphurs, *Doing Church,* 66.

[6]Ibid, 67.

instruments prohibited, but pews, air-conditioned buildings, microphones, and hymnals acceptable, although none of these things are mentioned in the New Testament?

What seems to be a much more logical and sensible way of using scripture to guide our worship practices is a "positive hermeneutic," which "argues that though a practice isn't found in the Bible, we are free to perform it as long as it doesn't differ with or contradict in any way the clear teaching of Scripture."[7] The application, of course, is that churches are free to use instruments in worship, even though there is the perception that they are not mentioned in the New Testament, but more importantly, because the teaching of Scripture does not prohibit them.

Obviously, much of this debate concerning the negative hermeneutic is irrelevant, as I have shown in pillars three and four that instrumental music is, in fact, referenced in the New Testament, specifically in the implied references in Ephesians 5:19 and Colossians 3:16, and the references to heavenly worship in the book of Revelation.

---

[7] Ibid, 69.

Chapter 7
Historical Considerations

Denominational Traditions that Prohibit Instrumental Music in Worship

Two of the more conspicuous denominations that prohibit instrumental music in worship are the Reformed Presbyterian Church and the Church of Christ. The decision to remove instrumental music from the worship of the Reformed Presbyterian Church goes all the way back to the Reformation,[1] while the Church of Christ did not emerge as a denomination until 1906.[2] Both denominations cite

---

[1]Bruce C. Stewart, "Churches that Refrain from Use of Instruments in Worship" in *Music and the Arts in Christian Worship,* ed. Robert Webber, Vol. 4, Book 1, *The Complete Library of Christian Worship* (Peabody, MA: Hendrickson Publishers, 1994), 438.

[2]Thomas H. Olbright, "Churches of Christ" in *The Encyclopedia of the Stone-Campbell Movement* (2004).

the same reason for the exclusion of instruments from their worship. For the Reformed Presbyterians, it is called the regulative principle: "Worship is to be offered only in accordance with God's appointment, and in harmony with the scriptural principal (sic) that whatever is not commanded in the worship of God, by precept or sample, is forbidden."[3]

The Churches of Christ actually separated themselves from their parent denomination, the Disciples of Christ, because of their opposition to the use of instruments in worship.[4] The reason cited for this opposition is basically the same as the Reformed Presbyterian's regulative principle, though more specific in its focus: The Churches of Christ "are seeking to worship according to the instructions of the New Testament. The New Testament leaves instrumental music out, therefore, we believe it right and safe to leave it out, too. If we used the mechanical instrument we would have to do so without New Testament authority."[5] This principle is the negative hermeneutic, discussed previously in chapter 6.

Both of these denominations point to the "historical evidence for absence of instruments in

---

[3]Stewart, "Churches that Refrain from Use of Instruments in Worship," 438.

[4]Olbright, "Churches of Christ."

[5]Joe R. Barnett, *The Churches of Christ... Who are These People?* (Lubbock, TX: Pathway Publishing House, 1979), 9.

the early church,"[6] and one leader in the Reformed Presbyterian Church even goes so far as to say, "There is neither command nor example given by Christ or the apostles of the use of instruments in worship.... Musical instruments are no longer needed or appropriate."[7] Is this really an accurate analysis of the early church's position on instrumental music, and if so, what factors might have contributed to this perception?

The Early Church

The early Christian church worshiped in a variety of places, including the Temple, in synagogues, and in house churches. Jesus and his disciples worshiped in the Temple (Matt. 21:23, John 8:20, Acts 3:1), as did the apostle Paul (Acts 21:26), so "There is every reason for us to believe that the Jewish Christians of Jerusalem continued to take part in Temple worship as long as the Temple stood."[8]

Extending to the time of Jesus, the Temple was a place of instrumental music, but the early

---

[6]Everett Ferguson, "Instrumental Music" in *The Encyclopedia of the Stone-Campbell Movement* (2004).

[7]Stewart, "Churches that Refrain from Use of Instruments in Worship," 438.

[8]Joseph F. Green, *Biblical Foundations for Church Music* (Nashville: Convention Press, 1967), 127-128.

synagogues were not.[9] This contrast is primarily due to instrumental music's association with temple sacrifices, and the fact that sacrifices did not take place in synagogue worship. The only exception to this exclusion of instruments was the use of the shofar, or ram's horn, which only served as a signaling instrument.[10]

Early Christian worship was greatly influenced by the synagogue worship tradition, and this continuity with the synagogue service included the absence of instrumental music.[11] Writers on early church worship, though, cite many other reasons for this exclusion of instrumental music.

Musical instruments were traditionally associated with practices that were detestable to early Christians, including pagan worship and heretical Jewish sects.[12] One writer even suggests that musical instruments were associated with sexual immorality and prostitution.[13] Because of

---

[9]Edward Foley, *Foundations of Christian Music: The Music of Pre-Constantinian Christianity* (Collegeville, MN: The Liturgical Press, 1996), 56.

[10]Ibid, 57.

[11]Susan J. White, *Foundations of Christian Worship* (Louisville, KY: Westminster John Knox Press, 2006), 47.

[12]Donald P. Hustad, *Jubilate II: Church Music in Worship and Renewal* (Carol Stream, IL: Hope Publishing Company, 1993), 149.

[13]James McKinnon, "The Meaning of the Patristic Polemic Against Musical Instruments," *Current Musicology* 1 (1965): 69-70.

these immoral associations, early Christian leaders felt an obvious "need to wean the increasing numbers of converts away from everything which reminded them of their pagan past."[14]

Perhaps the most convincing reason why musical instruments were not a part of the worship of the early church has to do with the nature of their gatherings. As C. F. D. Moule points out, "Though the Temple had elaborate choirs with instrumental accompaniment, the poor and frequently clandestine Christian assemblies can hardly have boasted instruments."[15] Very often, these were small gatherings, in private homes, similar to modern small group Bible studies. These groups most likely did not have the resources for the support of instrumental music, nor did they want to call attention to themselves during a time of intense persecution. As Paul Jones points out, "Trumpets and cymbals tend to draw attention, something that Christians in hiding would undoubtedly strive to avoid."[16]

The persecution of the early church is thoroughly documented in the book of Acts: Peter and John were arrested (Acts 4:1-3), the apostles

[14]A. Joseph King, "Praise the Lord with the Sound of the Trumpet," *The Church Musician,* October 1982, 8.

[15]C. F. D. Moule, *Worship in the New Testament* (Richmond, VA: John Know Press, 1961), 65.

[16]Paul S. Jones, *Singing and Making Music: Issues in Church Music Today* (Phillipsburg, NJ: Presbyterian and Reformed Publishing Company, 2006), 27-28.

were jailed (Acts 5:17-18), Stephen was stoned to death (Acts 7:54-60), Saul persecuted the church (Acts 8:3), James was put to death and Peter imprisoned (Acts 12:1-4), Paul and Barnabas were persecuted (Acts 13:50), the apostles were threatened with stoning at Iconium (Acts 14:1-6), Paul was stoned and presumed dead (Acts 14:19), Paul and Silas were imprisoned (Acts 16:22-24), Jason was threatened (Acts 17:5-9), and Paul was seized in the temple and beaten (Acts 21:27-33). With this intense threat of persecution hanging over the early church, most of their meetings were secretive and virtually silent. The use of instruments in their worship services would have called unwanted attention to their gatherings and jeopardized the lives of those early Christians.

Other factors that contributed to the absence of instruments in the early church were the fact that instruments were very primitive and performers relatively unskilled. As James Ode contends, "Widespread acceptance of instruments in the service... was not achieved until instruments were developed and performers skilled to a degree approaching the beauty of vocal music."[17] Joseph Green even goes so far as to say, "Where instruments were not used, the lack of talent may have been the major factor."[18]

The instruments that the early Christians were

---

[17]James Ode. *Brass Instruments in Church Services* (Minneapolis: Augsburg Publishing House, 1970), Preface.

[18]Green, *Biblical Foundations for Church Music,* 129.

familiar with in worship were the instruments associated with temple worship, and King reminds us that they were owned by the Temple and consequently stored there, so they were not readily available to the people of the early church.[19]

The possibility remains, though, that Christians may have employed personal instruments in their small gatherings. There is an indication that the church in Ephesus may have, in fact, used a harp in their worship services. This possibility is suggested by evidence that their Bishop at the end of the second century, Polycrates, was known to have the symbol of a harp on his signet ring.[20] While other early church leaders chose a dove or a fish as their symbol, it is significant that the Bishop of Ephesus chose a harp, particularly in light of Paul's admonition to the church at Ephesus: "Talk to one another in psalms and hymns and spiritual songs. Sing and play to the Lord from your heart."[21]

Despite all these limitations on the early church's use of instrumental music in worship, as the church grew and Christianity became an accepted religion, and as musical instruments developed and Christians became skilled performers, the use of instruments has become a

---

[19]King, "Praise the Lord with the Sound of the Trumpet," 8.

[20]John Foster, "The Harp at Ephesus," *The Expository Times* 74 (October 1962-September 1963): 156.

[21]Markus Barth's translation of Eph. 5:19, *Ephesians* in *The Anchor Bible* (New York: Doubleday & Company, Inc., 1974), 554-555.

vital and accepted part of Christian worship. This widespread use of instrumental music in worship today is clearly supported by the biblical foundations outlined, both in the Old and New Testaments, beginning with the Psalms and music in the Davidic tradition, continuing through the implied references in Paul's epistles to the Ephesians and the Colossians, and culminating in the references to heavenly worship in the book of Revelation.

Appendix 1
Glossary of Terms

Ark of the Covenant - The wooden chest or box in which the Israelites kept the two stone tablets containing the Ten Commandments.

Family of instruments – A grouping of related instruments (i.e. woodwind family, brass family, percussion family, string family).

Instrumentalist - A person who plays on a musical instrument.

Levites - Members of the tribe of Levi, from which assistants to the Jewish priests were chosen.

Mishnah - The collection of interpretations and discussions of the Law of Moses by the rabbis, codified about 200 C.E.; oral law of the Jews. The Mishnah is written in Hebrew and forms the basic part of the Talmud.

Negative hermeneutic – Because something is not found in the New Testament it is inherently wrong and unbiblical.

Offertory - The music sung or played while the offering is received.

Pentateuch - The first five books of the Old Testament: Genesis, Exodus, Leviticus, Numbers, and Deuteronomy.

Positive hermeneutic – Because something is not expressly forbidden in the New Testament, the church or denomination is free to operate under the lordship of Christ and the freedom of the Spirit of God.

Prelude - A composition played at the beginning of a church service.

Psalm heading or ascription – Title that appears before the majority of the psalms, indicating a variety of references: authorship, relationship, occasion of the psalm's composition, designated use of the psalm, desired musical effect or setting, or basic character of the psalm.

Psalter – The book of Psalms.

Regulative principle – Whatever scripture does not command is forbidden.

Talmud - A collection of 63 books containing the

body of Jewish civil and canonical law derived by interpretation and expansion of the teachings of the Old Testament; the Mishnah together with the Gemara, which was completed about 500 C.E.

Appendix 2
Instruments in the Psalms

Psalm Ascriptions

1. <u>Psalm 4:0</u> For the choir director; on **stringed** instruments. A Psalm of David.

2. <u>Psalm 5:0</u> For the choir director; for **flute** accompaniment. A Psalm of David.

3. <u>Psalm 6:0</u> For the choir director; with **stringed** instruments, upon an eight-stringed **lyre**. A Psalm of David.

4. <u>Psalm 12:0</u> For the choir director; upon an eight-stringed **lyre**. A Psalm of David.

5. <u>Psalm 54:0</u> For the choir director; on **stringed** instruments. A Maskil of David, when the Ziphites came and said to Saul, "Is not David hiding himself among us?"

6. <u>Psalm 55:0</u> For the choir director; on **stringed** instruments. A Maskil of David.

7. <u>Psalm 61:0</u> For the choir director; on a **stringed** instrument. A Psalm of David.

8. <u>Psalm 67:0</u> For the choir director; with **stringed** instruments. A Psalm. A Song.

9. <u>Psalm 76:0</u> For the choir director; on **stringed** instruments. A Psalm of Asaph, a Song.

Psalm Texts

1. <u>Psalm 33:2</u> Give thanks to the LORD with the **lyre**; Sing praises to Him with a **harp** of ten strings.

2. <u>Psalm 43:4</u> Then I will go to the altar of God, To God my exceeding joy; And upon the **lyre** I shall praise Thee, O God, my God.

3. <u>Psalm 45:8</u> All Thy garments are fragrant with myrrh and aloes and cassia; Out of ivory palaces **stringed** instruments have made Thee glad.

4. <u>Psalm 47:5</u> God has ascended with a shout, The LORD, with the sound of a **trumpet**.

5. <u>Psalm 57:8</u> Awake, my glory; Awake, **harp** and **lyre**, I will awaken the dawn!

6. <u>Psalm 68:25</u> The singers went on, the musicians after them, In the midst of the maidens beating **tambourines**.

7. <u>Psalm 71:22</u> I will also praise Thee with a **harp**, Even Thy truth, O my God; To Thee I will sing praises with the **lyre**, O Thou Holy One of Israel.

8. <u>Psalm 81:2-3</u> Raise a song, strike the **timbrel**, The sweet sounding **lyre** with the **harp**. Blow the **trumpet** at the new moon, At the full moon, on our feast day.

9. <u>Psalm 92:3</u> With the **ten-stringed lute**, and with the **harp**; With resounding music upon the **lyre**.

10. <u>Psalm 98:5</u> Sing praises to the LORD with the **lyre**; With the **lyre** and the sound of melody.

11. <u>Psalm 108:2</u> Awake, **harp** and **lyre**; I will awaken the dawn!

12. <u>Psalm 144:9</u> I will sing a new song to Thee, O God; Upon a **harp** of ten strings I will sing praises to Thee,

13. <u>Psalm 147:7</u> Sing to the LORD with thanksgiving; Sing praises to our God on the **lyre**,

14. <u>Psalm 149:3</u> Let them praise His name with dancing; Let them sing praises to Him with **timbrel** and **lyre**.

15. <u>Psalm 150:3-5</u> Praise Him with **trumpet** sound; Praise Him with **harp** and **lyre**. Praise Him with **timbrel** and dancing; Praise Him with **stringed** instruments and **pipe**. Praise Him with loud **cymbals**; Praise Him with resounding **cymbals**.

Appendix 3
The Devotional Series

The Biblical Foundations of Instrumental Music in Worship – Four Pillars
by Dr. Brian L. Hedrick

Note to the instrumental director: This four-part devotional series is designed for you to present in your group rehearsals, over four consecutive weeks. Each devotional is only three to five minutes in length, and can simply be read to your group during a break in the rehearsal. Please read and study the material yourself before presenting it to your instrumental groups. It is my prayer that it will be a blessing to your ministry!

Introduction to the Series (read with week one devotional):

As Christians, we are a people of the Book, but

as we devote ourselves each week to praising the Lord with our instruments, are we clear on what the Bible says about the subject of instrumental music in worship? If we were asked to provide biblical support for the instrumental music ministry in our church, do we understand all that the Bible has to say on the subject?

The biblical foundations for the use of instrumental music in Christian worship are found in four distinct areas in Scripture. These "four pillars" will be presented in the form of rehearsal devotionals over the next four weeks, as we seek to understand the biblical basis of what we do each Sunday, leading our congregation in worship.

A. Week One/Pillar One – The Psalms

The first pillar in the biblical foundations of instrumental music in worship is the Psalms. When considering the Psalms and instrumental music, most instrumentalists think of Psalm 150, but there are actually a total of twenty-four psalms that mention the use of instruments in worship, either in the psalm heading or in the text itself. We won't take the time to examine all those psalms, but let's take a closer look at two of the more familiar psalms that mention musical instruments, Psalm 150 and Psalm 33.

Psalm 150 concludes the book of Psalms with a chorus of praise, including every family of instruments: woodwinds, brass, percussion, and strings:

Praise Him with *trumpet* sound;
Praise Him with *harp* and *lyre.*
Praise Him with *timbrel* and dancing;
Praise Him with *stringed instruments* and *pipe.*
Praise Him with *loud cymbals*
Praise Him with *resounding cymbals.*
(Psalm 150:3-5)

Pipe, trumpet, timbrel (or tambourine), cymbals, harp, lyre (similar to the harp), and stringed instruments, representing all four families of instruments and all used in praise of almighty God! Even though this psalm mentions instruments in each of the four families, note the conspicuous absence of singing. Commentators on this psalm have seen this as undeniable biblical support for instrumental praise alone.

Psalm 33 is the first psalm to mention instruments, and connects the worship attitudes of joy, thanksgiving, and praise with the use of instruments:

Sing for joy in the Lord, O you righteous ones;
Praise is becoming to the upright.
Give thanks to the Lord with the lyre;
Sing praises to Him with a harp of ten strings.
Sing to Him a new song;
Play skillfully *with a shout of joy.*
(Psalm 33:1-3)

Take special note of the latter half of verse three in this particular psalm: "Play skillfully with a shout of joy." We are to play skillfully as we worship the

Lord. The famous British preacher, Charles Spurgeon, comments on this verse, "It is wretched to hear God praised in a slovenly manner. He deserves the best that we have." Let us remember this biblical mandate to minister with excellence each and every Sunday!

Next week, we will examine pillar two of the biblical foundations for instrumental music in worship: Worship in the Old Testament under King David, otherwise known as Davidic worship.

B. Week Two/Pillar Two – Davidic Worship

Closely related to instrumental music in the Psalms is the use of instruments in the worship practices of King David, or "Davidic worship." This is the second pillar in the biblical foundations of instrumental music in worship.

King David is called "the sweet psalmist of Israel" in 2 Samuel 23:1. On top of that, he is the most frequently mentioned individual in the psalm headings throughout the book of Psalms. David is also largely responsible for the Old Testament tradition of instrumental music in worship, which began as he ascended the throne of Israel, and extended to the time of Christ.

Prior to King David, worship in ancient Israel was relatively silent, largely without the use of instruments. Beginning with David's reign as king, though, there was an explosion of instrumental music, as evidenced in a wide variety of passages in 2 Samuel and 1 Chronicles. In 1 Chronicles 16,

David formed a small orchestra of eight strings, two trumpets and one cymbal player to accompany the worship before the Ark of the Covenant. Seven chapters later, in 1 Chronicles 23, this orchestra seems to grow to four thousand players! How's that for tremendous orchestra growth? Actually, some biblical scholars think that figure may be an exaggeration on the part of the writer of Chronicles. Others feel that the Hebrew word, translated "thousand," is more accurately understood as a clan or group. In 1 Chronicles 25, a more reasonable orchestra of twenty-five players is listed, closer in size to what we are accustomed in our worship.

The group of Israelites appointed by David as instrumentalists were from the tribe of Levi. These Levites were ancient Israel's worship leaders, responsible for the care and transportation of the wilderness tabernacle and all its furnishings under Moses. Once the Tabernacle and the Ark of the Covenant were in their final resting place, the Levites' job description changed. They were no longer the moving crew for the Tabernacle. Instead, David set about training the Levites to sing and play instruments, and then set them apart for the service of the Lord through music. 1 Chronicles 25:1 and 6-7 says:

Moreover, David and the commanders of the army set apart for the service some of the sons of Asaph and of Heman and of Jeduthun, who were to prophesy with lyres, harps, and cymbals; All these were under the direction of their father to sing in the house of the Lord, with cymbals, harps and lyres, for the service of the house of God. Asaph, Jeduthun and Heman were under the direction of the king. And their number who were trained in singing to the Lord, with their relatives, all who were skillful, was 288 (there's that word skillful again!).

After the reign of King David, there were periods of moral and spiritual decline, followed by times of revival under kings like Hezekiah and godly leaders like Nehemiah. With these times of revival, worship was restored in the manner of King David, and that always involved the use of musical instruments. You can read about this in 2 Chronicles 29, Ezra 3, and Nehemiah 12.

Finally, one of our goals, when we gather each week for worship, is to glorify God and seek his presence among us. When Solomon dedicated the first Temple, he did it with musical instruments in the tradition of his father, David. In 2 Chronicles 5:11-14, we read:

> And when the priests came forth from the holy place (for all the priests who were present had sanctified themselves, without regard to divisions), and all the Levitical singers, Asaph, Heman, Jeduthun, and their sons and kinsmen, clothed in fine linen, *with cymbals, harps, and lyres*, standing east of the altar, and with them *one hundred and twenty priests blowing trumpets* in unison when the trumpeters and the singers were to make themselves heard with one voice to praise and to glorify the Lord, and

when they lifted up their voice accompanied by *trumpets and cymbals and instruments of music*, and when they praised the Lord saying, "He indeed is good for His lovingkindness is everlasting," then the house, the house of the Lord, was filled with a cloud, so that the priests could not stand to minister because of the cloud, *for the glory of the Lord filled the house of God.*

The Temple dedication service reached its climax when the instruments and singers were unified in praise of almighty God, and God, in turn, put his stamp of approval on the gathering by filling the house of God with his glorious presence, in the form of a cloud. Let us, as instrumentalists, seek to be unified in our praise, as we glorify God and seek his presence!

Next week, we will examine pillar three of the biblical foundations for instrumental music in worship: Implied references to instrumental music in two familiar New Testament worship passages.

C. Week Three/Pillar Three – New Testament Implied References

We have established that there are abundant references to instrumental music in the Old Testament, specifically in the Psalms and under the Davidic tradition of worship, but what about the New Testament? Some denominations claim that there are no references to worship with instruments in the New Testament, and since we are under the

New Covenant, we should not use instruments in Christian worship, but is this really true? Let's look closer, by examining two familiar New Testament worship passages, which are pillar three in the biblical foundations of instrumental music in worship.

> Speaking to one another in psalms and hymns and spiritual songs, singing and making melody with your heart to the Lord; (Ephesians 5:19)

> Let the word of Christ richly dwell within you, with all wisdom teaching and admonishing one another with psalms and hymns and spiritual songs, singing with thankfulness in your hearts to God. (Colossians 3:16)

Notice that both of these passages encourage the use of psalms in worship, and what have we learned in pillar one about the use of the Psalms? Many of them are associated with the use of musical instruments, either through the psalm headings or direct references in the text. The most notable one is Psalm 150, with its reference to all four families of instruments. Through this link to the Psalms, we see that both these passages contain an implied reference to the use of instruments in worship.

As we look a little closer at the latter half of Ephesians 5:19, we discover an even more direct reference to using instruments in worship. The apostle Paul, who wrote both Ephesians and Colossians, says that we should sing and "make melody" with our heart to the Lord. The Greek word, translated "make melody" in the NASB, is *psallo.* The original meaning of this word is "to pluck the strings of an instrument." In fact, one of the most respected commentators on the book of Ephesians, Markus Barth, translates this verse, "Talk to one another in psalms and hymns and spiritual songs. Sing *and play* to the Lord from your heart." This is more than just an implied reference to instrumental music; it almost sounds like a direct command to praise God with instruments!

Finally, let us examine the context of the verse in Colossians, by looking at the verse that follows it, Colossians 3:17: "And whatever you do in word or deed, do all in the name of the Lord Jesus, giving thanks through Him to God the Father." *Whatever* you do, including playing an instrument, can and should be done in the name of the Lord Jesus, with a thankful heart.

Next week, we will examine our final pillar of the biblical foundations for instrumental music in worship: Instrumental music in the book of Revelation.

D. Week Four/Pillar Four – The Book of Revelation

Did you know that the book of Revelation contains more instruments by name than the rest of the New Testament combined? Instrumental music in the book of Revelation, therefore, is the fourth pillar in the biblical foundations of instrumental music in worship.

Harps are mentioned three times in Revelation, the same harp that was associated with worship under King David and with the singing of the Psalms. In fact, the harp or the lyre (a form of harp) is the most frequently mentioned instrument in the entire Old Testament. The three passages in the book of Revelation all depict harps in the heavenly worship of the victorious Lamb of God:

> And when He had taken the book, the four living creatures and the twenty-four elders fell down before the Lamb, *having each one a harp*, and golden bowls full of incense, which are the prayers of the saints. (Revelation 5:8)

> And I looked, and behold, the Lamb was standing on Mount Zion, and with Him one hundred and forty-four thousand, having His name and the name of His Father written on their foreheads. And I heard a voice from heaven, like the sound of many waters and like the sound of loud thunder, and the voice which I heard was like *the sound of harpists playing on their harps*. (Revelation 14:1-2)

> And I saw, as it were, a sea of glass mixed with fire, and those who had come off victorious from the beast and from his image and from the number of his name, standing on the sea of glass, *holding harps of God*. And they sang the song of Moses the bond-servant of God and the song of the Lamb. (Revelation 15:2-3a)

The other instrument mentioned repeatedly in the book of Revelation is the trumpet. Just as the harp in Revelation had its foreshadowing in the Old Testament, this trumpet is the same trumpet that was used by the priests in ancient Judaism. This time, though, it is the seven angels in Revelation 8, announcing the seven judgments of God.

So as we examine instrumental music in the book of Revelation, we see harps accompanying heavenly worship, and trumpets used in fanfares, heralding God's revelation. These are two distinct functions in worship that can be applied in our churches today. We accompany worship, in the form of choir and congregational accompaniments, while instrumental preludes and offertories herald God's revelation.

One final point must be made, based on this clear picture of worship in the New Testament: If instrumental worship is acceptable in heaven, then why not on earth? Our limited worship on this earth is but a preparation for our occupation in heaven, and if we base that on the biblical model in Revelation, it should include the use of musical instruments for his glory!

Sources Consulted

Alcorn, Randy. *Heaven.* Carol Stream, IL: Tyndale House Publishers, Inc., 2004.

Allen, Leslie C. *1, 2 Chronicles* in *The Communicator's Commentary.* Waco, TX: Word Books, 1987.

_____. *Psalms 101-150* in *Word Biblical Commentary.* Waco, TX: Word Books, 1983.

Atkerson, Steve, ed. *Ekklesia: To the Roots of Biblical House Church Life.* Atlanta: NTRF, 2005.

Aune, David E. *Revelation 1-5* in *Word Biblical Commentary.* Dallas: Word Books, 1997.

_____. *Revelation 6-16* in *Word Biblical Commentary.* Nashville: Thomas Nelson Publishers, 1998.

Bale, Peter. "Brass Bands and the Salvation Army." *Brass-Forum.co.uk.* http://www.brass-forum.co.uk/Articles/BrassBandsintheSalvation Army.htm (accessed August 10, 2007).

Barnett, Joe R. *The Churches of Christ... Who are These People?* Lubbock, TX: Pathway Publishing House, 1979.

Barth, Markus and Helmut Blanke. *Colossians* in *The Anchor Bible.* New York: Doubleday & Company, Inc., 1994.

Barth, Markus. *Ephesians* in *The Anchor Bible.* New York: Doubleday & Company, Inc., 1974.

Bauer, David R. *An Annotated Guide to Biblical Resources for Ministry.* Peabody, MA: Hendrickson Publishers, 2003.

Beale, G. K. *The Book of Revelation: A Commentary on the Greek Text* in *The New International Greek Testament Commentary.* Grand Rapids: William B. Eerdmans Publishing Company, 1999.

Braun, Joachim. *Music in Ancient Israel/Palestine: Archeological, Written, and Comparative Sources.* Grand Rapids: William B. Eerdmans Publishing Company, 2002.

Caird, G. B. *A Commentary on the Revelation of St. John the Divine* in *Harper's New Testament Commentaries.* New York: Harper & Row, Publishers, 1966.

Caram, Daniel G. *Tabernacle of David.* Longwood, FL: Xulon Press, 2003.

Collier, Richard. *The General Next to God: The Story of William Booth and the Salvation Army.* New York: E. P. Dutton and Co., Inc., 1965.

Conner, Kevin J. *The Tabernacle of David.* Portland, OR: City Bible Publishing, 1976.

Corbitt, J. Nathan. *The Sound of the Harvest: Music's Mission in Church and Culture.* Grand Rapids: Baker Books, 1998.

Craigie, Peter C. *Psalms 1-50* in *Word Biblical Commentary.* Waco, TX: Word Books, 1983.

Cranfill, Jeff. Interview by author, 21 August 2007. Email.

Curl, Charles E. "Developing a Theology of Worship to Inform the Use of Musical Instruments." D.Min. dissertation, Drew University, 1961.

Douglas, Winfred. *Church Music in History and Practice: Studies in the Praise of God.* New York: Charles Scribner's Sons, 1962.

Duncan, Jon. "Biblical Foundations for Instrumental Music Ministry." In *The Instrumental Resource for Church and School,* ed. Julie Barrier and Jim Hansford, 13-25. Nashville: Church Street Press, 2002.

Dunn, Steve. "Praise Him With... Instruments!" *Creator: The Bimonthly Magazine of Balanced Music Ministries,* September/October 2001, 4.

Faulkner, Quentin. *Wiser Than Despair: The Evolution of Ideas in the Relationship of Music and the Christian Church.* Westport, CT: Greenwood Press, 1996.

Fensham, F. Charles. *The Books of Ezra and Nehemiah* in *The New International Commentary on the Old Testament.* Grand Rapids: William B. Eerdmans Publishing Company, 1982.

Ferguson, Everett. "Instrumental Music" in *The Encyclopedia of the Stone-Campbell Movement* (2004).

Foley, Edward. *Foundations of Christian Music: The Music of Pre-Constantinian Christianity.* Collegeville, MN: The Liturgical Press, 1996.

Foster, John. "The Harp at Ephesus." *The Expository Times* 74 (October 1962-September 1963): 156.

Frame, John M. *Worship in Spirit and Truth.* Phillipsburg, NJ: Presbyterian and Reformed Publishing Company, 1996.

Gage, John. Interview by author, 11 September 2007. Telephone.

Gelineau, Joseph. *Voices and Instruments in Christian Worship.* Translated by Clifford Howell. Collegeville, MN: The Liturgical Press, 1964.

Green, Joseph F. *Biblical Foundations for Church Music.* Nashville: Convention Press, 1967.

Grenz, Stanley J. *The Baptist Congregation.* Vancouver, BC: Regent College Publishing, 1985.

Hall, Harry Hobart. "The Moravian Wind Ensemble: Distinctive Chapter in America's History." Ph.D. diss., George Peabody College for Teachers, 1967.

Henry, Matthew. *Matthew Henry's Commentary on the Whole Bible*. Vol. 6, *Acts to Revelation*. McLean, VA: MacDonald Publishing Company, 1985.

Hallquist, Gary. Interview by author, 22 August 2007. Email.

Hill, Andrew E. *1 & 2 Chronicles* in *The NIV Application Commentary*. Grand Rapids: Zondervan, 2003.

_____. *Baker's Handbook of Bible Lists*. Grand Rapids: Baker Books, 1981.

_____. *Enter His Courts with Praise! Old Testament Worship for the New Testament Church*. Grand Rapids: Baker Books, 1996.

Hoehner, Harold W. *Ephesians: An Exegetical Commentary*. Grand Rapids: Baker Academic, 2002.

Holz, Ronald W. *Brass Bands of the Salvation Army: Their Mission and Music*. Hitchin, England: 2006.

Hustad, Donald P. *Jubilate II: Church Music in Worship and Renewal*. Carol Stream, IL: Hope Publishing Company, 1993.

Japhet, Sara. *I & II Chronicles: A Commentary* in *The Old Testament Library.* Louisville KY: Westminster/John Knox Press, 1993.

Jones, Paul S. *Singing and Making Music: Issues in Church Music Today.* Phillipsburg, NJ: Presbyterian and Reformed Publishing Company, 2006.

Keil, C. F. *1 and 2 Kings, 1 and 2 Chronicles* in *Commentary on the Old Testament.* Edinburgh: T & T Clark, 1872. Reprint, Peabody, MA: Hendrickson Publishers, 1996.

Kidner, Derek. *Psalms 1-72* in *The Tyndale Old Testament Commentaries.* London: Inter-Varsity Press, 1973.

_____. *Psalms 73-150* in *The Tyndale Old Testament Commentaries.* London: Inter-Varsity Press, 1975.

King, A. Joseph. "Instrumental Music in Southern Baptist Life." *Baptist History and Heritage* 19.1 (January 1984): 46-54.

_____. "Praise the Lord with the Sound of the Trumpet." *The Church Musician,* October 1982, 4-8, and November 1982, 16-19.

Kirby Steve. Interview by author, 21 and 23 August 2007. Email.

Kirkland, Camp. Interview by author, 11 September 2007. Email.

Kirkpatrick, A. F. *The Book of Psalms* in *The Cambridge Bible for Schools and Colleges.* Cambridge: Cambridge University Press, 1921.

Koivisto, Rex A. *One Lord, One Faith.* Wheaton, IL: Victor Books, 1993.

Leithart, Peter J. *From Silence to Song: The Davidic Liturgical Revolution.* Moscow, Idaho: Canon Press, 2003.

Leonard, Richard C. "Psalms in Biblical Worship." In *The Biblical Foundations of Christian Worship,* ed. Robert E. Webber, 244. Vol. 1, *The Complete Library of Christian Worship.* Nashville: Star Song, 1993.

Liesch, Barry. *People in the Presence of God: Models and Directions for Worship.* Grand Rapids: Zondervan Publishing House, 1988.

Malphurs, Aubrey. *Doing Church: A Biblical Guide for Leading Ministries Through Change.* Grand Rapids: Kregal Publications, 1999.

Mayo, Lawrence William. "Full-time Programs of Instrumental Music in Nine Selected Southern Baptist Churches." DMA diss., Southern Baptist Theological Seminary, 1986.

McKinnon, James. "The Meaning of the Patristic Polemic Against Musical Instruments." *Current Musicology* 1 (1965): 69-82.

Metro Instrumental Directors Conference. "MIDC Adopts Mission Statement." *Bulletin Board* Opus 1, No. 1 (June 1995): 1.

Metro Music Conference. "Requirements and Invitation Procedures." Adopted 12 February 1986.

_____. "Metro I Membership Qualifications." Approved at the 1997 Metro I Conference, Dallas, TX.

Montagu, Jeremy. *Musical Instruments of the Bible*. Lanham, MD: Scarecrow Press, 2002.

Moravian Music Foundation. "The Moravian Church." http://www.moravianmusic.org/MMchurch.html (accessed August 10, 2007).

_____. "Moravian Music." http://www.moravianmusic.org/MMusic.html (accessed August 10, 2007).

Moule, C. F. D. *Worship in the New Testament*. Richmond, VA: John Know Press, 1961.

Mounce, Robert H. *The Book of Revelation* in *The New International Commentary on the New Testament.* Grand Rapids: William B. Eerdmans Publishing Company, 1977.

Mowinckel, Sigmund. *The Psalms in Israel's Worship.* Grand Rapids: William B. Eerdmans Publishing Company, 2004.

Music, David W. *Instruments in Church: A Collection of Source Documents.* Lanham, MD: Scarecrow Press, 1998.

_____. *With Stringed Instruments... Or Not?* www.lifeway.com (accessed July 18, 2005).

Ode, James. *Brass Instruments in Church Services.* Minneapolis: Augsburg Publishing House, 1970.

Olbright, Thomas H. "Churches of Christ" in *The Encyclopedia of the Stone-Campbell Movement* (2004).

Pirner, Reuben G. "Instruments in Christian Worship: A Historical-Theological Perspective." *Church Music* 70.1 (1970): 1-7.

Quasten, Johannes. *Music and Worship in Pagan and Christian Antiquity.* Translated by Boniface Ramsey. Washington, DC: National Association of Pastoral Musicians, 1983.

Reynolds, I.E. *Music and the Scriptures.* Nashville: Broadman Press, 1942.

Sachs, Curt. "Music in the Bible," in *The Universal Jewish Encyclopedia,* 1942.

Seel, Thomas Allen. *A Theology of Music for Worship Derived From the Book of Revelation.* Metuchen, NJ: The Scarecrow Press, Inc., 1995.

Sendrey, Alfred. *Music in the Social and Religious Life of Antiquity.* Cranbury, NJ: Associated University Presses, Inc., 1974.

Sims, W. Hines. *Instrumental Music in the Church.* Nashville, TN: Sunday School Board of the Southern Baptist Convention, 1947.

Sproul, R. C. *A Taste of Heaven: Worship in the Light of Eternity.* Lake Mary, FL: Reformation Trust Publishing, 2006.

Spurgeon, Charles H. *The Treasury of David.* Vol. 1, *Psalm 1-57.* Peabody, MA: Hendrickson Publishers, 1988.

Stapert, Calvin R. *A New Song for an Old World: Musical Thought in the Early Church.* Grand Rapids: William B. Eerdmans Publishing Company, 2007.

Stewart, Bruce C. "Churches that Refrain from Use of Instruments in Worship." In *Music and the Arts in Christian Worship,* ed. Robert Webber, 438-439. Vol. 4, Book 1, *The Complete Library of Christian Worship.* Peabody, MA: Hendrickson Publishers, 1994.

Stott, John R. W. *The Message of Ephesians* in *The Bible Speaks Today.* Downers Grove, IL: Inter-Varsity Press, 1979.

Werner, Eric. "The Conflict Between Hellenism and Judaism in the Music of the Early Church." *Hebrew College Annual,* Vol. XX (1947): 407-470.

White, Susan J. *Foundations of Christian Worship.* Louisville, KY: Westminster John Knox Press, 2006.

Williamson, H. G. M. *Ezra, Nehemiah* in *Word Biblical Commentary.* Waco, TX: Word Books, 1985.

Willis, Charles. "Instrumental Music Enhances SBC Outreach." *Arkansas Baptist Newsmagazine,* 11 August 1983, 2.

Winkler, David. Interview by author, 17 August 2007. Telephone.

_____. "Remembrances of the Early Metro Conferences." *25th Anniversary Metro Instrumental Directors Conference Notebook.* Cruise to Miami, Key West, and Cozumel: May 3-7, 2004.